Hole

Acknowledgements

Appreciation as always goes to my family, friends and fellow writers for their loyalty and support, especially Sarah, Leah, Rachael, Mary, Pauline and Jeremy.

Thanks also to the editors of the following publications where versions of some of these poems were first published: *Aireings, Fire, Iota 76, Iota 81, Hudson View Poetry Digest, Other Poetry, Purple Patch, Reach, Red Ink, Roads,* and *The Journal.* An additional expression of gratitude goes to Gordon Smith whose encouragement all those years ago contributed to the development of this collection.

Hole

Kathleen Kenny

Published 2009 by
Smokestack Books
PO Box 408, Middlesbrough TS5 6WA
e-mail : info@smokestack-books.co.uk
www.smokestack-books.co.uk

Printed by
EPW Print & Design Ltd

ISBN 978-0-9560341-1-3
Smokestack Books gratefully
acknowledges the support of
Arts Council England

Smokestack Books is
represented by Inpress Ltd
www.inpressbooks.co.uk

These poems are dedicated to the memory of
my father Jim (1899-1976),
and my brother Jimmy (1941-1968).

Did you see ya Da while you were out?
We passed.

Contents

Reverberations

I am crammed in with white plastic,
sweat running down my teeth
as I head for the coast on the Metro.

Crossing the river my legs shiver,
echoes stepping from the staithes
slide me down to Dunston.

Other times and lives,
clattering tongues and eyes,
a long dark dress, rough and heavy.

The river's scum under high water:
the gristle of a smile, twisted
wrought iron.

Tracks the coal trucks left
still there, glittering
under the moon.

The banks of the Tyne are slime
green, black, green again.

Something wet climbs out
louder than a train.

182 Westmorland Road

We are looking up at roof tiles on 180,
painting in next door's wraith,
tracing dusty names on this window,
the only pane of glass left intact.

My daughter wants to break in,
to seek out shadows
from 182's doppelganger kitchen,
to see what it was really like
back then, imagine

there is water boiling
and a light is on in every room
and upstairs the midwife is delivering
me, her mother, to her grandmother,

and to entertain the older children
her granddad is making rabbits
appear on the wall over the warm
cast-iron mantelshelf,

and there really is a big soft brush
sweeping away years of ash
from the centre of the hearth,
from this fantastic house,

from where our beginnings lead.

Blue House

One year on from meeting, a son
is born, a man becomes a father;
a flame takes hold in winter blue.
Wedding cutlery provides the knife
to ice a cake in this wartime house:
white welcome for a first-born's life.

And this is where we all come alive:
three daughters, one precious son;
to congregate in this house,
under the roof of our father,
learning how to hold a knife,
a fork, a spoon that tips us up, tinges us blue.

Standing on our heads in sailor blue
in the high-ceilinged rooms where we live
like pirates, our dressing up games, knife
at the hip, between our lips; the sun
glinting on the blade: prayers to Our Father
Who Art in Heaven. Hallowed be this house.

Our Victorian dad, his Victorian house,
mysteries both, and blue/
black as the best coal our father
lights. How can we live
after all, without fire, and a son
to carry on the line? Then comes the knife.

No one sees it. No one talks of it. Knife
is not mentioned, but slices our house
softly, muting the tongues of son
and father, until dumb as bluebells
we come to accept the way we live:
accommodate the silence of our father;

the muffled grumbles of our father,
his tongue a sheathed knife.
And Jimmy, our brother alive
but quiet, withdrawn to the attic of the house
with the company of his own eyes. Blue
inheritance of the only son:

father's image and likeness, as they cross the house,
blue blades shimmering. This strange normality: knives
in the morning sun of our weekday lives.

Irish Stew

Boiled onions, tender meat,
taties soft as the Host.
It was the normal course
yet there was an oddness to us.

Dad insulting his own:
You can take an Irishman
out of the bog, but you can't
take the bog out of an Irishman.

The sayings and jokes I recollect
though not which meal it was
the last time they spoke:
Dad.   Son.
Please pass the salt.

Slum

Plastic doorbells are swank.
They light up and are musical.

Ours has a big cold metal pull
that doesn't work.

All the servants are all dead.
Just rattle the letterbox.

29 Warrington Road

When the darkness comes
spectres root in our street
breaking through the ground
curling banisters,
wrapping round our feet.

Mam writes to her sister,
letters in the dark.
We hang starched dresses,
our cravats without a crease
with hats that haven't breathed for years.

In the blue kitchen
lino tiles come to life.
A disco gets underway
as they sway from the skirting,
pour into the holes from Mary's stilettos.

Black-clocks in trouser suits
dancing 'til the break of day.

The Non-spoken Word

Too many kittens, not enough mousers:
This lot are gannin in the pail.

Laid out in the bin
warm ashes resuscitate them.

Now Dad must drown them again.
I throw Jupiter in the tatie bag and run.

Jimmy flies up to his room
with a pile of jam and bread.

He's remembering the tot
they said he pushed in

that hot bank holiday.
Dumb. No one knows anything.

He was six then, Dad seventeen
when the First War silenced him.

Great Wars and small tragedies.
Secrets from before my birth.

Unknown sadnesses I came among,
buried like dead kittens

then resurrected,
then reburied.

Me and Jimmy in a Hole

They are seen at such distances,
summer ghosts

at Whitley Bay, you in the big sand
digging the best hole ever:

so deep you can stand up to your chest.

I'm the little pest, jumping in
disturbing its tight-packed surface

receiving a slap on the way down,
treading your feet to make myself tall

before you crumple me
with your new-manly hands

then spread your arms over the sand,
smirk for the camera.

We're in that hole together
no matter what they say.

We're in that hole together.
I'm down there with you.

All the way.

The Drowning

Swept from the river bank,
one deck-hand flying
frantic finger-flags.

Skull and crossbone rags
half-mast, no rescue.
No more pirates, only aftermath.

Slipped or pushed, how did he fall?

Not all of us, eh, shipmates?
Not all. *Only Jimmy. He did it.*

Under questioning Jimmy said nothing.
Nothing for thirteen years on drowning.

Then, looking back, he was asked
if he recalled the Healy boy,

the accidental fall from childhood:

Yes. He said.

Yes. I did.

The Small Drum

Lost while out at play
that Saturday in May 1947:
Terence, only child of Mr and Mrs Healy.

His toy drum found at 5am next day
on Skinnerburn, near some steps
leading down to the water.

Recovered face down, opposite
wharf 23, his body was conveyed
to the Swing Bridge mortuary

where his father identified
the three-year-old boy
as his one and only son.

His blue and white striped shirt,
blue pullover, brown check trousers,
white socks, and sandals

were fastened and orderly. No sign
of violence on the body which appeared
to have been in the water about ten days.

There was no evidence to show how he came
to be in the water: Terence, only child
of Mr Healy, occupation: window cleaner.

Icicles

Those useless articles

flaunting themselves as we freeze,
taunting us from attic windows,
dangling off the eaves.

Our Brother reaches up, risks his skin
for the most alluring
diamond daggers;

formations that fall from him,
tasteless
and most beautiful.

***

Inside, the slow thaw
demands patience, not blow lamps,
the risk of burst pipes.

Dad's tools have seized.
He's toasting his backside,
reprising that tale about the man

who tells his son to jump
from the top of a ladder
into the safety of his arms.

Then, when the lad does as bidden
the man moves aside
and his son hits the ground.

Let that be your first lesson in life,
the father says, trust nee one
not even yer own fether.

***

We scrape our nails across flakes
of ice inside the window.
Our Jimmy is out the back.

We watch him wrap
a massive icicle
in a dirty white hanky.

He licks the bumpy surface
then puts it in his pocket
like pirates' treasure.

Did Dad tell him that yarn,
I wonder? Did they ever talk,
spend time with one another?

How fast the distances.

How fast he goes

pulling the freshly buttered sledge
from the back yard shed
hoping no one has seen him.

The Cupboard under the Stars

The wardrobe opens on gloves, shoes, hats,
saddlebags for the horses.
We tie them up and slip into the saloon
tell the bartender to set 'em up.

I am a cowgirl, or Rowdy Yates.
The beds are mountains we negotiate.
It's hard to cross soft mattress pass
and carpet waves are treacherous.

We make the floorboard plains,
draw the curtains to bring in night.
In a table cave we set up camp,
or brave it under the stars,

where, after a bellyful of buffalo meat
we dance with the kitchen mop.
(It's the only man on the trail
and he doubles up as cook.)

There is a sing, the crickets listening in,
then rest. In the morning old Whiskers
fries us beans and sausages
while we chew the cud

before remounting, heading off.

The Evils

Let's make pastry, and gravy,
feed it to the dolls,
spoon it into Dorothy's tight mouth:
watch her grimace, watch it cake.

Let's sit them in front of Quatermass and the Pit
or the Wednesday Play
where that woman gets a gun shoved in her face:
Swallow this you bitch!

Her lips round the nozzle. And the gold fish
I didn't mean to kill. My Brother's pet
lathered up, placed in a jam-jar to dry.
And the stray he named Jupiter.

Yes, it could be from a star
or a planet full of cats
but swung by the tail it screams
just the same. Squeals for mercy. Helpless.

Dancing with Ice

Jimmy's boiler suit on the backyard line
iced into a full-blown man.
I take him down, slide him
over the kitchen floor, past the big white sink
through the passage door
to the living-room hearth where we hug
go in circles, glow.

Without my Brother's innards
I can hold him by the waist
converse with his limbs,
whisper to his headless face:
Do you like to dance like this?
Then softened by the fire's heat
watch him melt. Escape.

Scrapheap

You want too much

must leave the chess set,
the maps, the population stats
and all your dreams of travel.

Let the card tricks slip away
for a practical trade
in the shipyards of Wallsend.

Your high school, like Dad's,
was on secondary mod hill,
where there's no point

in knowing where Borneo is.
But great that you showed me
before my class geography quiz.

All their faces stunned.
Me, a momentary star.
Though not half as smart

as you my clever Brother,
who will never go far,
will never travel further,

will never get beyond
Berwick's border.

Saver

You cultivate tobacco stains
from a Kensitas cigarette
as podgy yellow clouds
fill the upper deck.

On the wet ceiling of the number five
I write in brown with an index finger,
drawing in and out with crowds
of workers and other school kids.

You have a clean haversack
and navy overalls
and a job I know nothing about.
I am in a tie and grey pinafore.

You pretend not to know me, but think
about that scooter you are saving for
and the day you'll be able to ditch this bus
and never offer me a lift.

And one day I will exchange
all the tab coupons you have stacked
in neat piles under your bed
for a mustard breadbin and a dish-rack.

And like moving statues
life's bad habits will sneak up.
We don't see them yet
smoking away.

The Boy with Bitten Nails

You take a piece of wire
and twist it round your finger

and you twist it
and twist it

until your finger flies off
across the room
takes someone's eye out.

Then we celebrate,
make toasts to compensation claims

and you act like Dave Allen
become all comedic and unashamed
waggling the stump in front of the cameras

proud and good looking
like a true dark Irish wag.

Townies at Corbridge

Dad's Sunday knees are shot,
his veins, the strain on the legs
as he walks round the village grumbling.

Mam worries about her heels
sinking into the grass, stains
on her stockings. *Climb this hill.*
Take a run and jump, she says.

He wants a caf' for tea and tabs,
she wants fresh cream scone with jam.
We want pop and a sweetshop.

At the river we eat ice-cream, mimic ducks.
We watch sheep, and munch grass. Strange sights:
cows stretched out, Mam and Dad relaxed.

On the way home I force Dad into a piggy back.
His legs are tired. He's countried-out
but I'm best at nagging
Please Dad, please Dad, please Dad, please...

He gives in. I'm as tall as a mountain
bouncing on his shoulders
crossing the distance back to the train.

That distance
step by step.

That distance
breath by endless breath.

Triumph

When the motorbike comes
the push bike goes the distance,
though he keeps the flat cap as protection,
that, and the drink.

Keep Left, it says, go right, he thinks,
comes in grinning, carrying a headlamp,
snapped wires, a cake-slice of upper lip.

As we slide corners I cling,
blackening my socks on oily chrome,
number plates kept fastidiously filthy.

Other kids have short walks,
fathers with cars and new-fangled fridges.
I have distances, a Dad in dark leather gauntlets.
And a petrol cap shaped like a star.

Work

His eyes are hard as hazel nuts,
weathered.

The sun is in his ears,
warm, leathered.

A pocket of blue nestles
on his torn jacket

rests on an oil-can stain
settled on his sleeve.

The sky in him
is chopping wood, and singing.

The beast in him
is rasping like a rusty wheel.

Toolscape

Old tins:

candles, petrol,
sawdust, rust,
brushes, hardboard,
padlocks, dust,
plaster, putty,
turps and paint,
paper, oil, sand, cement.

The smell of things:

bootlaces, glue,
soles, nails.
A last: its iron feet
cast off
in all directions.
Chaplinesque.
Master of silence.

Him. My Dad.

Pliers

Here are pliers.
They come in.
Here they are
in plastic bags

full of old things,
Catholic things:
a 1921 florin found
in a secret drawer.

More pliers.
You never know
when they'll come in.
Pliers, full of the joys of spring.

Pliers, champion.

The Clothes We Lay Down In

Our icicle legs are unimpressed
by the fire's feeble efforts.
We all lie about freezing
in jumpers, top-coats, socks,

waiting to see what's fetched
to the table. Will the taties be boiled,
roast or mashed, will the meat impress
Dad, or be condemned as *auld mutton?*

We're starving and it's not
coming fast enough. How long
until the plates are brought
hot and heavy laden,

until we haul ourselves up
to the meal table, hoping
the door won't go again
with more *giddy-guys*

looking for cheap rooms?
Dad wants gents,
people who will pay their rent,
not more down-and-outs

who can only guess
where the next meal's coming from.

The Landlord

Many keys, many doors,
through passageways and halls,
to kitchens, yards and sheds.

Places where things are stored,
one where his motorbike is kept
in the middle of a room.

Walking in with him
I feel famous,
try to hold my breath,

keep out the smells
of damp and sweat,
stale dinners and debt.

Tenement Strangers

Before these properties were confiscated under compulsory
purchase orders Jim owned several tenement-houses in Elswick.

Everywhere there are locks
except on the bathrooms.

Creeping through makes me
nervous, constipated.

These houses of strangers
who sleep standing up

listening to downstairs voices
talking to themselves

or singing. They don't mind
being alone, but like

the impression of company.

Chimney Fire

At the bar of the Vic and Comet
Amber Ale and a gob of phlegm
force some colour into his sawdust skin,
put a glow on his cheeks and chin.

And here is our door, where she waits
for him. Her spruce face tight and sober,
shiny as a wax leaf.
Our grey slate roof rising with heat.

The sky a smokestack.

Valentino

He has a tea-towel on his hair
a rose between his teeth

six pints of romance
coursing through his feet

racing him home
to see her.

A Right Pair

She hangs her blue-flock night-coat
on the back of the bedroom door.

He folds her
into him.

They skip like ankle socks
in the first white breath of spring.

Houdini

He was brought up to accept
any priestly request
no question.
And attending Sunday Mass
doesn't seem unreasonable
at least not to our Mam who prays for it
or to us who have no choice,
who just want to be left
stretched in front of the TV set
with Saturday wrestling
and the prospect of the week's best tea:
chips with sausages, sausages with chips.

But here he is, the priest
like bliddy clockwork,
muscling in, being offered tea,
rubbing his happy hands and knees
as if this will conjure up Dad;
while Mam falls over backwards
to excuse the absentee:
he's just slipped out the back
two minutes to oil the locks,
unbolt the latch, free the catch,
release the chain
make his escape.

Old Battlegrounds

He's in a good mood, has just returned from
one of his spur of the moment trips to the continent
where he ditched his small travel bag
when it got too hot. Out went his body shirt
and long-Johns, even his cap. They all sailed out
through the train's open window,
over fields, vineyards, scarecrows,
left dangling there on telegraph poles.

At the village barber shop he told Jacques
to: *Take it all off,* came back to us
completely bald; a Neapolitan slice:
white crown, pink forehead, brown face and neck.

As a boy in Yprés his thick black hair
was mud-caked and cropped. Some young men
it's said, turned white. The average survival time
in the trenches being only four months.

He was lucky to be shot, sent for two years
to an army hospital down south
where he developed a party trick:
making the loose flesh inside his wrist dance.

In Northern France he lets it all go, recites
Rabbie Burns: *Man's Inhumanity to Man.*
The hot breeze dries his face
carries his underclothes across the French greens.
He is fifty-nine-years old. Free at last.
Nothing today is regulation. Even his head,
bald, and beautiful, being blessed,
being stroked by air.

Woodbines and Oranges

Grey clumps of phlegm,
these rhubarb clouds
tinged with yellow dust.

This view of Paris
tobacco and canvas
where he once stood

blowing smoke-rings
over the town
so quiet

and the sky a riot
of pinks, apricots,
blood-red oranges.

***

After the AWOL incident
Jim missed the Fusiliers' ship
was sent to the trenches
with a North Riding regiment
among whom he spent his war
gathering the lifelong opinion:
only a Yorkshire man knows
how to peel an orange in his pocket.

Hole

There's a hole in the road emitting sparks,
Dad parks himself at the edge,
beckons us over to take a neb.

Other people start gathering too,
clustering noses up to the stoup,
poking their eyes over the rim, gawping.

There are men down there in overalls
with picks and rakes, and pneumatic spades
and griddled gates that double as seats.

There are small men with beefy shoulders,
their heads bound with knotted handkerchiefs,
and a whippet in a wheelbarrow.

And underneath, a storm-drain feast
of gold and green and indigo slate
and chalky pinks and tricksy silvers

and slimy chains in rusty links
and huge black cobbles with long grey stumps
extracted like rotten wisdom teeth.

More people come, the hole gets bigger.
The entire day passes,
a fizz of oil, bubbles of gas.

At dusk a lamp like a parasol
throws light on nails lodged in wood,
sparkles of glass, old coins, winking coals.

Every lost place and thing glimmering.

Women hold out drinks to the dayshift
as they climb out grained and exhausted.
Then the nightshift pile in, with torches

and lanterns. And a candle-white horse,
tools in its saddlebags, its feet
shod with luminous hide, is lowered.

Then Dad takes hold of the mighty hod
packed with ancient stone and new baked brick
and his spine curves from the weight of it,

but his muscles shine like smiling cups
and he holds the hod up, hard as rock
all the way down to the molten core.

Lead-bottomed Boats

He is stretched out
on the orange couch
exhausted
from hammering nails.

His hands rest
across his chest
like a concert pianist's.
They are elegant: artworks.

When he wakes
from this unintended nap
he will be startled
by a moment of sunshine

startled by his light legs,
their lame attempts
to lift his entombed feet
back down to the floor.

These heavy boots
keep him leaded, earthed,
keep him wedded to the street
to the mundane tasks at hand.

Except for sleep
he wouldn't dare,
he wouldn't dare
allow himself to drift.

Boots of War

Up to the bicycle clips
up to the helmet.

Human rust nourishing mud.
Particles of water, particles of dust.

Boys in trench warfare.
The soft shit of Yprés

in their boots, the squeeze of leather
as snow drifts

into the slits
through the taties in their socks.

Quick boys, quick.

A bullet through the wrist
gets Jim out of it.

He's lucky. More than lucky.

Yet the battlefield's mist
will envelop his bed

soldering itself to his worn head
for sixty more winters

all under the same moon
where he is nothing but a leaf

trembling
falling to the ground.

Bedroom Minus Gallbladder

Moving curtains, cut-glass floor,
a new fire smoking, eating swirls
of paper from my Father's claw.

My Mother is bathing a new scar.
At her feet he has lain his great-coat
full of the secrets of war.

About the War

We are back into autumn
and it's cold.

I am curling a thread of hair
round your drowsy old ear lobe.

There is a bone inside your throat:
this funny thing called Adam's Apple.

It makes me mistake you
for someone who will tell.

Ambition

In my last school year I see myself
with a Saturday job in a shoe shop
earning enough to buy a bolero top.

Nothing will be beyond my imagining:
I will leave my future kids, Kate and Kerry
at the *Drop 'em and Shop Nursery*

while I go on my way, rich and free
to smell a variety of wardrobes in IKEA,
let the pleasures of wood-smoke reappear,

and mixing cement. What delight,
me and me Da, toiling like soldiers
towards our diplomas as master builders.

4 Hillside

Council and neighbour
versus Dad's hard labour:
the shed has to go.

Dougie owns next door's beard
and vista, and knows how to
twist a wrist to get his own way.

And it's true Darras Hall is
a bit of a leg up
from the back lanes of Elswick

where there are no views to spoil,
no garden parties with proper cups,
pea soup or tin-foil spuds

baked on Eileen's bonfire;
only jumpy-jacks and giddy-guys,
bangers and sky-high blazes.

Our Da says that here
they don't know what a hoose is.
Here, *it's aall bangalow, bangalow.*

Here, after years raising his status
from labourer to master builder
his mooth still has nee plums.

Despite his success, many hooses to let
there's some ill-wind in the air:
hints of compulsory purchase,

forebodings of T Dan Smith, Poulson,
what ever else is out there.
The fair crack of the whip he'll not sniff.

If only we'd had an American fridge,
lived on The Rise and been called O'Malley,
some romantic dally with another name.

Lord of all Hopefulness

When Jim built a house at 4 Hillside, Darras Hall, we moved out
of Elswick, and above our station. It didn't last. We moved back.

Our new house, five years or more
in the anticipation. Those Sunday visits
to the plot. The hut that was the hub,
with tin-cup-tea and sweet tinned milk.

Climbing ladders we saw the beginnings
of the first floor, got almost, almost,
nearly to the top,
before we lost our faith and toppled off.

Original Features

Our Victorian streets will soon be flattened,
chosen for demolition by the skewed vision,
greed, and high position of T Dan Smith.

Unlike the East End the West will not escape,
to be preserved or renovated. Our ceiling roses
will never be praised, nor our cast-iron ranges,
nor our door knobs, or our marble mantels.

All must hail the first expanse of scrub
where collective high-rise slums
will replace what they maintain
are our individual ones.

Like wars which create distinctions
where there are none. People will
be named Heroes on the one hand,
nonentities on the other.

The always dumb.
The Cannon Fodder.
The dumb, of whom my Dad is one,
of whom Dad knows all about.

Decanonized

It knows nothing:
my head is like a map
flat with lines,
drawings of the past.

It happened in 1969:
St Christopher they said
did not exist. At least
there is no proof of it.

Under compulsory purchase
our land is worth only sixty pounds,
our buildings worthless:
confiscated, flattened.

We live on the wrong side of town.
Inventors of nothing.
We don't know how to speak.
We can't articulate.

We are the banished smokers
of our time. We fume silently,
drink
to free speech and candour.

It happened in 1969:
St Christopher they said
did not exist. But we knew
nothing of it.

The patron saint of travellers
demolished, bull-dozed
like our West End homes,
all of Elswick.

So what remains of what we own
is ignorance and medals.

Memory Party for 182

We will sit on rotting mattresses
and the last remaining tufts of grass

mourning and drinking to our long gone home,
eating tongue of gargoyle, and Irish stew

issued with unused tokens from old ration books.
Ideas will form after a few

and a three part wooden ladder will be brought
to test the feasibility, the strength of next door's walls.

By late afternoon an order will be placed
for sixty-five bags of plaster and cement.

Then twelve rolls of gilt will descend
and eighteen lengths of cast iron railing

and a drum roll will commence
to announce the reconstruction

as we begin to reattach ourselves
to the last remains of this fine old house of Elswick.

The Reckless Sleeper

Dead shells and bullet holes. Earth empty
under tombstones
                              set to commemorate
the innocent sleepers: the seventeens dying
for a future.

He pulls the old army blanket over himself
as if it's all he has, drags his head to a rock,
a stone-white bolster.
                              He places his body
in a floral box like a jewel under lock
as his mind wanders off

into the underworld:
warfare in a blitz of light
                              across the blue midnight.

Lying twenty-four hours in no man's land,
the bullet through his arm lodged
                              in his thigh.

His shattered limb slowing it down,
                              saving his vital organs.

In the trenches of his dreary eyes
                              normal things present:
A cap, a razor, crows as big as cannons.

He dreams of ribbons wrapped round his claw,
 envisions them wound through
                              a girl child's hair.

Man with Newspaper in Morning Room

Behind his head privet curls as he reads the morning papers,
engrossed in the political assessments of The People,
The Pictorial: their incisive commentaries on current events.

With each saucer of tea the smoky sky grows thicker,
green velour steers to the floor, veers over Corky our Persian
who waits by the empty grate for fire.

What makes the man so still, so almost invisible?
It's a riddle. What goes up the chimney down
but not down the chimney up?

Why did the chicken cross the road?
What's black and white and red all over? He's a riddler.
A riddle behind his own door, in his own home.

This man who inhabits this house. He bought it.
He owns it. He is often there roaming the ground floor.
Yet even his boots on the parquet floor are a mystery:

on the one hand, all self-repair and careful cobblery,
all Stanley knife cuts on the other.
The slits he makes in his new leather boots,

which allow, he maintains, his corns to breathe.

The Impossible Healing

After Magritte

Because he is old and has remembered at last how to cry
they have opened up the iron gate to let out the black dove
that stands in place of a heart, crushed, all these years.

But it is misshapen now, and sits forlorn and quiet.
It has forgotten how to fly, so hobbles
behind the open door. It doesn't know how or why

it should now be free,
or see any reason for him to weep.
Except that he is full of fear, and demented.

256 Westmorland Road

The old worn steps,
high misshapen privet.
The times they fell in it:
our men.

It was dangerous back then.
A trip to the chip shop,
you could get lost,
not know where you lived,
where you belonged,
where you came from.

Just taking the top off
a bottle of pop,
washing a glass,
poking the coal fire:
things could explode
for no reason.

The Haunting of 256

Here they are:
cupboard skeletons
with roll-ups,
grimacing
as blue smoke
swirls into
their nose holes.

We keep doors shut
and shutters open,
pretend not to smell it,
concentrate
on the loaf of bread
at the centre
of the meal table.

Jimmy, Giving up for Lent

Aniseed Twist
        Hazelnut whirl

treats   you saved
     in that tempting tin.

A good Catholic boy
you never gave in.

No displays
until at last the moment
               came:

the end of abstinence,
the fizz of Sherbet Lemons

sweet breath

       tang

        of metal

the oven door
you put your head in.

The weight of your neck
soft
        on the shelf

of dead offerings.

Climber

I reach the bedroom on the first floor
lie on my goose-feather bed,
think of the floor above my head:
the back attic where you lived

until that last skirmish with Dad
saw you put out.
Your room, where I tiptoe to,
to cry into empty shoes,

hear you on the bare stairs, two by two,
imagine you make the attic,
let yourself out onto the flat roof
from where taller buildings loom

storey upon storey upon storey,
with stair-flights unruly as splinters
and there is no tiring of banisters
or golden stair-rods, or grippers,

and endless rainbow paths
spin out, and a spiral staircase
which you pursue
stopping only when darker than dark

to pick up your torch-shaped star.

Dad as Sculpture

After the sculpture by Taratynov and Dronov of Rembrandt's
Night Watch

I take your massive hand cold and lined
and shake it like a gauntlet.
I crook it in my soft palm,
begin fingering your sleeve,
the elaborate stitching,
your doublet laced with crowns,
then your huge knees, and copper socks,
the bow-front Cuban heels, your helmet
and fleur de lys, your hose, your trouse,
the fancy knot at the back of your girdle.

Your boots are full of water
and overflowing lace,
flakes of coal have made indents
in your face, where in the early hours
you fell before the fire
cold and helpless,
dumb for all of us.

What use the sleeping nightshift,
picking bits of coal at sun up from your skin,
hoping the blood will flow back in?
What use to notice now how peeled you are
from lack of fluids? Or that you will not live
another week? Let's pretend you give me
one last chance sire, to correct this,
to serve you as a good daughter should.
Here Father, what can I do?
Let me dust your feather hat.

Dad from the Window of 256

I was hiding behind the curtain, looking out.
They'd tied you into a cold-white-metal chair

and were carrying you off
down the front steps to an ambulance.

You were wrapped in a in a red crocheted blanket.
It reminded me of that film *Marnie*
where anything red on anything white sends her crazy.

Don't put me beans on me mash.
No monkey's blood on me ice-cream cornet.
If anything touches it will all collapse.

Avoid the cracks
count to ten
don't breathe.

That fearful house.
That day.

My little coward heart
tearing.

Swanking Off

Caught at the airport with cheap tabs
they take my fingerprints in blood.

On the final leg of my travels
the bandages unravel.

A ticket man in the railway carriage
reminds me I am second class

and should never have sat outside Café Neon
eating Greek salad

imagining I belonged under a parasol
or on the fringes of café society.

My mythology was killing nits in Meths,
rescuing pigeons from drowning in the outside netty,

me Da ribbing me Ma:
Hey, kidda, this one thinks she's royalty.

My Parents with Coloured Hair

Hid in their wardrobe with moth balls
I poke my nose out to breathe, see my Mother
in the single bed snoring like a hoover.
A mustard candlewick covers the dreamy lump of her.
Her dishevelled hair just visible on the pillow.
Between their beds is an enamel pail one-third full
of piss. The fumes don't penetrate. She's used to it.

As I sneak out, the door creaks, and the floor,
but nothing affects them. Dad has a leg out.
He's in his combinations, only a white foot bare.
Next door, the girls' room:
I crane at the wall to listen.
They are wailing at the moon,
scaring the living daylights from each other.

Our Mary's been out at The Stoll Picture House.
Her first sight of the Count: D.R.A.C.U.L.A.
Me and my sisters enacting the roles:
Mary, Prince of Darkness,
me and Pauline with painted neck-holes;
too concerned with the undead
to dream myself up, years ahead.

The Season of the Dolls' House

Mother doll hoovers,
father doll strokes the black cat.
Four child dolls slide the banisters.
One is straddled half way down
while a lift waits to take them back to the top.
It smells of pine and liquorice
and announces itself like a squawking crow.

There is a mousetrap under the floor
and a tallboy fitted into a corner
and a finely finished cabinet
waxed with lavender polish.
There is porcelain and a companion set
and a brass fender and a fireguard
and a pie on a green plastic tablecloth.

If we blew it up into a full size home
we might understand what went wrong:
the water tank's lack of insulation,
the paltry heat from the sweet wrapper coal,
our failure to realise the value of light,
or the way we stare out
as if independent movement were a myth.

Trip to Cork with Long-dead Brother

So here I am with lipstick
and red palette

though time will turn me black

that young man still taps
inside my head

beneath the cataracts
his coquettish eyes peer out

and he says he's not dead
and that he wants out

his subterranean hands
drilling at my brittle bones

his youth still moist
stretched against the odds.

West Road Cemetery

Under the earth
a trail of silver light
opens the darkness
between my Brother's bones
and my Father's.

The pull of the earth
has sucked them close
but still they face opposite.

Now she too is part of it:
mother and wife, trouble and strife,
me walking about on top.
All my complaints and gratitude
out loud, like me Da.

Asking the three of them
to sort it out, at last
before I arrive.

Family Reunion

Being young once,
sitting in the green night
reading fortunes,
seeing fire split, divide,
making chasms between
what should be whole.

No one will leave
until it has been turned
over and over;
until the past is utterly dead.
Until all that remains
is dark white ash.

Afterword

In a sense, what our Pauline says is right:
For his eight remaining years
Dad lived a ghost life.
They both died together
on the same lonely night:
The night our Jimmy took his own life.